Poverty Must Persist

POVERTY MUST PERSIST

A collection of new poems by Kim Sayi
Translated by Sunnie Chae

POET

아시아

Contents

Stains	9
Rift	10
Clock-Out to Clock-In	13
Bodily Memory	16
Reprisal	17
Truth Is	19
Incomplete	22
Do Not Forgive	24
In a Nightscape	25
Moving to Seoul	27
Emotion Market	28
Purchasing Convenience	30
Memory	32
Extreme Job, Human	34
Under a Solid Roof	37

Knotted Emotion	39
Menopause	41
Dreamy Delusion	43
Labor Market	45
Sea of Suffering	46
An Ache	51
Poet's Note	53
Poet's Essay	57
Commentary	63
Praise for Kim Sayi	73

POVERTY MUST PERSIST

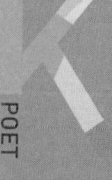

Stains

Sunlight, broken-winged, falls on a shanty town
Fallen sunlight fuels wind, struggling to soar
Struggle-fed sorrow seeps through nameless dreams
Tattered and threadbare, work starves and suffers
Sturdy thresholds for status but none for distress
Slick-tongued dealers in protest or support
Fearful disgust in places dampened by disgrace

Rift

A pipeline hole pulls in a technician
Scanty scaffolding makes a builder fall

No regular contract for security guards
No workplace benefits for janitors

Childcare and chores can't count as work
Cafeteria cooks can't count as workers

A med student's death is precious life lost
A teen mechanic, chalked up as labor loss

High-skilled work deserves top pay
Cheap labor, less than a living wage

Degrees give right to a salary
Others don't deserve job security

I proudly wear my lanyard ID
Hard-won badge of a full employee

I may have what you don't
You may never have what I don't

Playing fields stay unlevel
Unfairness is equal for all

Though AI may replace us

Work will continue, renewed

Pain will continue, repeated

Clock-Out to Clock-In

Commuters on foot and in cars

Weaved and unweaved

Yielding in turns at crossroads

I gazed from a rush-hour bus

Proud to be part of the scene

Unsteady on hungover legs

Squeezed in the sardined metro

Sprinting, desperate not to be late

Clocking in on time at my workplace

Those were diligent days

Supervisors bossed around

Colleagues badmouthed me

While I sought solace in my work
Even humoring superiors
Who wanted company for drinks
I meekly earned my pay

I complained feebly to friends
Vowed to quit in the morning
Changed my mind by the evening
Others have it harder, I thought
Collecting another check

Alike in more than lanyard ID
Huddled at lunch with coffee
Sharing woes in twos and threes

Was it all but a dream?

Offering my life to belong
Tossed away before long

Memory

Seasons spent sowing sesame, planting seedlings, harvesting tuber crops and rice; packed in a van with others at dawn, whisked away to vegetable fields; pain-relief-patched, toiling long for pittances; back braced, body hauled and dragged; farming, cooking, caretaking around the clock but never called by name; joints swelling, sweat running dry; laborious life ailing, pulse fading as loneliness sets in; sorry to be idle, nursing a body meant to die and rot; guilt-driven to apologize, sick or not; icy current of poverty clinging on like sin; work eaten away by work; work winding down near death; lifelong work missed most by overgrown tufts of grass.

Reprisal

Laid off from work
I trudged in the rain without cover
My office shoes and toothbrush
I tossed away to celebrate
The cheap send-off

Fired like a rubber band
An expendable commodity
Gone were all traces
Of my hard-earned sweat

The labor I performed
Where has it flowed?
Where has it landed?

Disposable masks that hid my fear

Are now discarded everywhere

Elastic loops, deadly avian snares

I live as you die

Things tossed now return

Myself thrown away

By throwaways

Products of capital

Convenience turned nuisance

Warning turned irreversible price

Truth Is

At twenty, I left for Seoul
A training institute referred me
To a company newsroom
I became a white-collar Seoulite
Pleased to work in an office
Though in godforsaken Guro
When I went home for holidays
Pa called me Assistant Kim
The title mattered

Boasting backfired
Neither a writer nor an editor
I was a coffee-serving errand girl
Cleaning the office, greeting guests

Miss Kim, Miss Kim, becked and called
Unmarried I was and surnamed Kim
But why was I the office drudge?
Irked and ired, I finally quit
You squared a wrong, I told myself
You spoke for justice, I insisted
Cleverly misleading the misled
To stroke my pride

My twenties, a corner shop
Crammed full of assorted vices
Clannish conceit, envy, avarice, and more
I cast blame on twentysomethings
Forgetting my arrogant passage

Through those brazen years

Now middle-aged and idle
I could serve coffee, send mail
Clean and empty bathroom bins
I accept chores and drudgery
But search for work in vain

Incomplete

Lifeless clocks hold time; famished, left to flatline

In drowning dreams
Bloodied longing gnaws
As someone else's time forever fuels my sweat

Your lean, hungry youth wears out working gigs

Hours scatter under light, no salary in reach; legs ache, lonely and out of time

Fed or not, no matter
I work while nearing menopause
Past the pain of monthly cramps

Period paused or complete

I must hold down unstable jobs

Unchanged, finite, ticking down

Do Not Forgive

Words on fingertips
Gnaw on verdant flesh

Mouths latch on like viruses
Eyes rob me blind

A child fed to beasts
Devoured to the bone

Away from vulturous gaze
The carcass finally warms

In a Nightscape*

I weep

Washing dishes

Sorting recyclables

City lights burn

Like love unrequited

Sated illusion

Spurs habit

Habit benumbs

As time carries me on

* Translator's note: the poem mourns those lost in the MV *Sewol* and October 29 crowd crush disasters.

To hear your face

To see your voice

I stay unstill

An alley lost

On a still day

Lingers long

Moving to Seoul

Like an accident, I found myself on a bus Seoulbound; my back to the hillside home among chestnut trees; in a seat surrounded by wafting odors and stale breath; skin crawling, stomach sickening, head throbbing in unfamiliar company; no one asked questions or cared to know; traveling to her mother, they assumed; queasiness quieted as my eyes warmed to sunlight; the sight of new scenes quickened my pulse; that day, an unknown future yanked my green roots; at the start of migrant life, I was new to motion sickness, moving to Seoul.

Emotion Market

You and I diverge
In forlorn ways

Loath to be lonely
You pay to smile, I to cry

Alone or in blessing
Born in human form
To live human lives

The simple path
Forked and divided
Some human, others beastly

Human animals

Live in solitary cells

Within and out safaris

Trading solitude

For currency

Buying yours

Selling mine

I pay to be lonely

Purchasing Convenience

As varied as forms of irregular work
Are the times, fees, emotions of deliveries

They alleviate my chores
Fees rise, drivers and riders are strained
But deliveries dash to all doors

A single click
Summons convenience

Glutted capital evolves

Workers age out or die away
We forget the forgotten with no apology

With no reflection, the forgotten we forget

Containers add to piles of plastic
But I purchased my rights for a fee

The pain convulsing your legs
Concerns only you, not me

Memory

Snowfall turns the square blue

Though I once played on snowy hills

Poor flesh and blood now shivers

Misfortune never misses prey

Water pipes and heaters crack

Hunger strikers shudder in tents

Life falters on hospital beds

Anxious eyes freeze above masks

Talks freeze in stalemate

Scar tissue hardens in wounds

Borrowed time expires

Lowly lives stiffen cold

Pain stays as the weather thaws

Aching like an age-old landscape

Helplessly blue

Extreme Job, Human

Being human or perhaps not
My despair reaches far back

I wandered eons before birth
Human kindness gave me breath

Malaise comes between humans
Exchanging painful blows

Are humans the world's oldest malaise?
Are humans the world's oldest future?

Countries rich and poor are beset
By storms of heat, rain, and snow

Conflicts civil and interstate
Disasters of weather and war
Humans shooting human faces
Young souls shattered and slain
The latest news breaks
And relieved to be safe
I take a vaccine to survive
Sorry to live and outlive
My face today, ashamed

Work tires but malaise stirs awake

My face tomorrow will be masked
Days displaced like manhole covers

Will flood over with malaise

Under a Solid Roof

Traveling far, my body ails
Despair clings to reeling legs
Like creditors clamoring to be paid

Turn out your pockets to prove they're empty
Write down the exact color of your soul
While the cheats and cheated are screened
Honest bodies, stripped bare, float adrift
Slipping on forms, falling down procedures
Whom do bureaucracies serve?

Refined, rational desire and flexible resolve
Serve to persecute the poor for being poor
Under the roof of this cushy kingdom

Would it be soft and warm to lie inside
Spacious, marble sarcophagi?

Long-suffered defeat reeks of a musty basement room
Long-suffered silence smells of a staggered cough
I trudge toward barbaric time
Biting on hardened sorrow

Knotted Emotion

Assigned to a girls' senior high in Gwangju, I become a self-boarding student; I rented a room from an elderly couple, distant relations of a hometown friend; before school started, my parents helped me move; they exchanged greetings with the elders and got up to leave; Pa stepped out and then Ma; I stopped at the gate, feet rooted to the ground, tears bursting as if my soul were ablaze; Ma stood still as I sobbed though who knows why I wailed; it was only my first parting, hardly a tragedy since I was no baby being weaned; the elders gawked, my roommate giggled, and renters peeked out their doors; Ma fixed me with a stare; who knows what she saw while waiting without a word; when my eyes and nose were finally dry, she turned, fading shadow and all into the sunset; being childless, I will never fathom the depths of that gaze; it reminds me of the glance she gave when I, as a child, almost ran away at night.

Menopause

Poetry replaced first love

as my partner in life.

I wrote as if dating,

as if keeping house.

They said poetry was song,

that mine did not sing;

they were not right or wrong.

Where did songs originate?

Sorrows weighty or light

left narratives to match.

Like a canary in a mine,

I lost traces of fight;

I saw myself, fearful.

Drunk on tears,

I mistook ditch for road,

wept, wrote, whooped, warbled

as tides washed over me.

I struggled on in age,

my sensibilities sagged

in selective decline.

I now inch deathward

and overstay my time.

I am stilled, stagnant.

Dreamy Delusion

Being together

at times emboldened,

at times instilled fear.

I practiced obedience

out of ignorance.

Scarred into patterns,

I woke up on thorns,

haunted by memories

stirring sickness.

I flinched as if burned,

shaking off and away

emotions that stained,

clinging like migraines.

For a brief connection

going out on a limb,

I painted over you,

you reassembled me,

staying out of step.

Whatever we were,

I was thrown out on the street,

bare fleshed to be devoured.

To some, perhaps a dream,

to others, feverish delirium

or something in between:

time faltering green.

Labor Market

Faith is faulty construction

Dreams, bread in a freezer

Work without the worker

Desire bellyaching, famished

Despair consumed in despair

Ambulances, routine like meals

Death addicted to daily life

Daily life addicted to death

Digging graves at work

Trapped by ties overtime

Sea of Suffering

There is no more rice. No money for rice. Four families, two families, one family go hungry. Without water or electricity before ending their lives.

Staying still only to drown.
Calling for help only to be crushed.

Newborn babies die without a trace. In trash bins, plastic bags, freezers. By the road or hiking trails. Some go missing; others are shipped abroad.

Children, beaten by parents and foster parents. Kept away from school. Starved of company and food, trapped indoors and left to die.

At home, daycare, and kindergarten, they suffocate under blankets, get pinched and bruised, or worse, they're maimed. Whole lives blighted.

Innocent, young lives. It takes a village to raise a child, but too many are killed instead of raised.

Mothers wither from parenting alone. They leave for work guilt-ridden as children cling on. They fall ill as wives or as women treated as playthings.

They're stabbed in bathroom stalls, struck down on streets.

Crashed by road ragers and drunk drivers. Killed, injured, and crippled with family.

Abused on dates. Robbed, kicked, dragged, and threatened.

Rewarded for office work by being made dinner escorts.

Builders fall from heights, die crushed under shipping containers, get caught and lose fingers in machines.

Delivery workers die of exhaustion.

Security workers are threatened, scorned, and humiliated, driven to suicide.

Loved ones die unattended, claimed by a virus.

No warmth to quell their fear or loneliness.

They pass unseen and return as handfuls of ash.

The dying and living are wronged.

I dread.

I dread war.

I dread people as much as war.

I dread words spat out.

I dread mouths that feed.

I loved less, wanted less, ached less.

Rice, our sustenance, deserves no discrimination. Will I be out of work today or tomorrow? My days alternate between anxiety and pain whether I try to sleep or wake. No retreat, no refuge. Can a new resistance bring about coexistence? Protesters carry on, but why do talks fall through? Can rational individualists unite, living together rather than dying? What is the rice that sustains me; whose lives does it touch? I wonder.

An Ache

Amid hard-pressed days

Weighted with despair

Bodies go unmourned

Workers who never returned

Children who never came of age

Fatalities repeated on end

Unending after death

Voices pierce through silence

While I survive to dig my grave

Leeches feed on their blood

The dead do not begrudge

With chameleon-like excuses
With well-wrapped apologies
The living gorge themselves full

No fall foliage for greenery
As winter follows summer
Each harrowing day godsent

In times past and times to come
Lives striving to live are lost
The violence around us stays

POET'S NOTE

Looking Back

Empty-handed and knackless
I resigned my young self to a bus

Sheer desperation

No dreams or delight
Not knowing what to do
Or how to survive

I was blunt and raw
With no keen eye
A novice in money matters
Without means to a living
I arrived in search of work

To feed my body and soul

Guro factory and shanty town
Sweatshop district of blue collars and Korean-Chinese
Here, Garibong
The many-named place
That passed me around
And rough-handled me

In the caged coop, I blended
But when I emerged
I saw my ragged self

Enamored with the death
Of poets who died young
I hummed "Seoul Moon"
And wallowed in sorrow

Full of childish conceit
Of living short and sweet

Instead of passing quicky
I stayed a thirty-year fixture
In Garibong, Guro

Today like yesterday
Tomorrow like today
I bow to my once-only day

POET'S ESSAY

There Lies the Sea

Shoulders seemingly shaken, I blinked my eyes open. Squinted in a daze. Blinded by light. Outside time and space. Walked without a path, shouted without sound.

I stepped blindly in place. Stood before a door. A wooden frame door papered with *changhoji*. The one from my childhood home. I had bored holes through the paper, gauged the scenes outside, and waited for people to arrive. One winter, I dreamed of the world beyond.

*

She pressed an eye against the peephole—her

heart nearly stopped. An eye, bloodshot. She tumbled down and dampened like a dripping song. Her throat ached and stung. Chills rushed down her spine; goose pimples ran over her skin. Whimpers echoed down the walls of the pitch-dark room.

Child, why the tears?
Mom, don't cry.

Wails and soothing words clung on.
It pained her. Without her knowing.

*

Winter deepened. Shadows of the city, blank faces scuttled by.
Symptoms by her side—what would they

become? Lost in thought, her memory faded within minutes; a burning kettle on the stove went unnoticed. Her eyes would gleam, murderous like a person possessed. As if she were nearing some other state of being.

*

She watched the sunrise from Mount Jiri's Cheonwang Peak but lost her way down. Fog shrouded the view. A thick haze, ashen like the back alleys of nightclubs, showed nothing beyond a step. With the hiking party nowhere to be seen, she was trapped.

Lost stragglers waited for the fog to lift. Their hands and feet shivered; their bodies chilled over time. Nervous worries punctured words. Voices rose to cast blame. Unfazed, she trailed off into her mind, where she sank into that firm sea of fog.

*

The sun fled far from the Earth. Briny wind brushed her hair. She questioned again. Why am I out here? Should we meet at all? Whatever will I say?

Huddled pines provided shade. There she hid and retched. Bitter bile surged. Her stomach swirled. She sat still. The sea breezed with a puckering taste. Clammy. Just like her days.

*

Unni, I knew they didn't love themself. Now I understand. The sorrow on their face. The door vanished from my dreams. They had been that door. A passage for weary souls. A child and a mother too. They saved me and left. I had been too full, bloated, weighed down. Though not meant for me, I grasped. Nothing but a selfish animal. This selfish mask, I should remove before it bleeds into feelings. I won't lose myself again. Unni, don't hold me back.

*

I climbed onto a bus. Yesterday's me staggered behind. Out the window, smoke billowed from a trash pile burning in the corner of a field. Grim soot pillared upward, devouring the winter sky.

Over the mountain peak lay an endless sea. Open like a mammoth mouth, a portal to the unknown. A boundless black hole, an exit to salvation.

COMMENTARY

"Narratives to Match" and Songs of Life

Park Hyungjun
(Poet and professor at Dongguk University)

Kim Sayi is a poet whose poetry solicits my regards. I have met her only in passing once or twice, but since reading her first poetry collection *The Day I Quit Regret* (Silcheon Munhaksa, 2008), I have sometimes found myself sending her silent regards. Certain people elicit a sense of affinity. In the case of Kim, her poems open my heart and enlist solidarity. I attribute this partly to similar pasts—her poems detail childhood years in the countryside, studies in a larger city, and later experiences in the outskirts of Seoul. What resonates with me the most, however, is her barefaced sincerity.

In this third poetry collection *Poverty Must Persist*, the poem "Knotted Emotion" relates Kim's experience of leaving home to attend high school in Gwangju. Her parents turn to leave after helping with the move; the poet-narrator sees them out but stops in front of the gate. Facing her mother's back, she bursts into tears though confused as to why. As a schoolboy, I had also left home to live with older siblings in Incheon. We moved back and forth between two impoverished neighborhoods: Sumuntong (meaning "Water Gateway"), where the Yellow Sea flooded over reclaimed land in the summer, causing backflow in kitchens, and Sudoguksan (meaning "Waterworks Bureau Mountain"), a poor hillside village. After each move, I would lose my way home from school in the labyrinth of shanties; I would wander late into the night in tears. Back then, so many people left hometowns to earn their living in cities, but they encountered only the urban outskirts stained with death and alienation. Their emotions knotted within, never to unravel.

As I prepared to write this commentary, I recalled one of Kim's guest appearances on a radio literary show. She had brought with her the sound of a wind chime. Metaphor notwithstanding, she carried in the sound like a physical object; to her, it was not a rhetorical device for embellishment but an extension of her sincere way of life. During the radio show, the poet shook clanging notes out of the wind chime; she apologized to the listeners for the forced, jarring sound. When hung from eaves, she explained, wind chimes swayed in the breeze and rang in soothing murmurs like a babbling brook. Kim shared her hopes for life and poetry that flowed as fluidly as water.

The poet-narrator of "Menopause" muses:

> Poetry replaced first love
>
> as my partner in life.
>
> I wrote as if dating,
>
> as if keeping house
>
> They said poetry was song,
>
> that mine did not sing;
>
> they were not right or wrong.
>
> Where did songs originate?
>
> Sorrows weighty or light
>
> left narratives to match.

Kim's poems resemble these "narratives to match." In capitalist societies, I tend to believe that even poetic language follows economic logic. Under capitalism, those deemed successful earn more than they work, as opposed to just as much as they work. The same applies to a poet's use of language: poetry must outperform the investment of thought and effort to ensure the poet's success. But not so with the honest Kim Sayi, who wishes to create only as much poetry as allowed by her life and labor. Others might consider her poems to be coarse sounds of bare life rather than songs; in my eyes, her "narratives to match" serve as canaries in coal mines, presenting signs of true and honest life reinforcing our humanity.

The poem "Under a Solid Roof" decries a society in which "Refined, rational desire and flexible resolve / serve to persecute the poor for being poor." Readers find poverty reeking under the roof of a cushy, capitalist kingdom. Even these scenes strike me as songs—beautiful melodies like canaries in mines coughing up blood, forceful tunes like blades of grass spearing through asphalt. Only Kim would detect the smell of defeat and silence long suffered by the poor. When she likens the stench of defeat to a "musty basement room" and the odor of silence to a "staggered cough," the figures of speech extend beyond rhetorical flourish, kindling the heartrending pain experienced only when life overlaps with poetry. I would dare to say such poems stand alongside the extremely vulnerable, joining them in singing of the pain endured in this world. The despairing yet steadfast poet inhales defeat and silence on her way toward capitalist society's "barbaric time." Thus the true and honest poet mounts her poetic protest against those who had argued that "poetry was song" and that hers "did not sing."

The poet-narrator of "Reprisal" leaves her job and walks out in the rain, tossing away her office belongings as if to "celebrate / The cheap send-off." On the street, she witnesses birds dying with their legs tangled in disposable masks, those "deadly avian snares." "Things tossed" trigger the poet-narrator's empathy as she recognizes herself as a similar throwaway. This arrival at empathy is part of the arduous process of performing what Kim captures in another title: "Extreme Job, Human."

Poverty Must Persist carries on the major themes of Kim's earlier collections *The Day I Quit Regret* and *They Say I Do Nothing*, shedding further light on female labor and the Guro Factory Complex in former Garibong. The resonance of her latest poems derives from the quietly steady voice reflecting on lives caught in poverty and toil—a voice cascading like water to poignant effect. In the line "Lifeless clocks hold time; famished, left to flatline" from "Incomplete," readers discern traces of anxious days lived by the poet, who admits in her "Poet's Note" to having "stayed a thirty-year fixture / In Garibong, Guro." Kim's poems offer a rare encounter with resounding odes to life and songs of labor. Such is the distinctive work of a poet who directs her utmost reverence and concern toward lives in precarious places.

PRAISE FOR KIM SAYI

POET

The poet's confession moves our society one step farther into a progressive realm. Her confessions allow us to relate to others, to think of many more others, and to expand the breadth of our empathy. She is the new warrior of our age.

> Moon Jongpil, "Poems of a Warrior and a Romanticist,"
> *Quarterly Sijak* (2019)

Kim Sayi's poems give utterance to the voices of female laborers, who are doubly marginalized by men and by capital . . . . In this age wherein no one wishes to be a laborer despite the labor they perform, the poet delves into vulnerable lives that most try to escape; from those sites, she draws out the language of female laborers hitherto buried in silence and testifies as a steadfast witness to the enduring essence of human life.

Roh Ji Young,
"Literature of the Hospice, Enduring Sites of *Minjung*,"
Silcheon Munhak (2011)

K-POET
Poverty Must Persist

Written by Kim Sayi
Translated by Sunnie Chae
Published by ASIA Publishers
Address 445, Hoedong-gil, Paju-si, Gyeonggi-do, Korea
(Seoul Office:161-1, Seodal-ro, Dongjak-gu, Seoul, Korea)
Tel (822).3280.5058
Email bookasia@hanmail.net
Homepage Address www.bookasia.org

ISBN 979-11-5662-317-5 (set) | 979-11-5662-638-1 (04810)
First published in Korea by ASIA Publishers 2023

This book is published with the support of the Literature Translation Institute of Korea (LTI Korea).

K-픽션 시리즈 | Korean Fiction Series

〈K-픽션〉 시리즈는 한국문학의 젊은 상상력입니다. 최근 발표된 가장 우수하고 흥미로운 작품을 엄선하여 출간하는 〈K-픽션〉은 한국문학의 생생한 현장을 국내외 독자들과 실시간으로 공유하고자 기획되었습니다. 〈바이링궐 에디션 한국 대표 소설〉시리즈를 통해 검증된 탁월한 번역진이 참여하여 원작의 재미와 품격을 최대한 살린 〈K-픽션〉 시리즈는 매 계절마다 새로운 작품을 선보입니다.

001 버핏과의 저녁 식사-**박민규** Dinner with Buffett-**Park Min-gyu**
002 아르판-**박형서** Arpan-**Park hyoung su**
003 애드벌룬-**손보미** Hot Air Balloon-**Son Bo-mi**
004 나의 클린트 이스트우드-**오한기** My Clint Eastwood-**Oh Han-ki**
005 이베리아의 전갈-**최민우** Dishonored-**Choi Min-woo**
006 양의 미래-**황정은** Kong's Garden-**Hwang Jung-eun**
007 대니-**윤이형** Danny-**Yun I-hyeong**
008 퇴근-**천명관** Homecoming-**Cheon Myeong-kwan**
009 옥화-**금희** Ok-hwa-**Geum Hee**
010 시차-**백수린** Time Difference-**Baik Sou linne**
011 올드 맨 리버-**이장욱** Old Man River-**Lee Jang-wook**
012 권순찬과 착한 사람들-**이기호** Kwon Sun-chan and Nice People-**Lee Ki-ho**
013 알바생 자르기-**장강명** Fired-**Chang Kang-myoung**
014 어디로 가고 싶으신가요-**김애란** Where Would You Like To Go?-**Kim Ae-ran**
015 세상에서 가장 비싼 소설-**김민정** The World's Most Expensive Novel-**Kim Min-jung**
016 체스의 모든 것-**김금희** Everything About Chess-**Kim Keum-hee**
017 할로윈-**정한아** Halloween-**Chung Han-ah**
018 그 여름-**최은영** The Summer-**Choi Eunyoung**
019 어느 피씨주의자의 종생기-**구병모** The Story of P.C.-**Gu Byeong-mo**
020 모르는 영역-**권여선** An Unknown Realm-**Kwon Yeo-sun**
021 4월의 눈-**손원평** April Snow-**Sohn Won-pyung**
022 서우-**강화길** Seo-u-**Kang Hwa-gil**
023 가출-**조남주** Run Away-**Cho Nam-joo**
024 연애의 감정학-**백영옥** How to Break Up Like a Winner-**Baek Young-ok**
025 창모-**우다영** Chang-mo-**Woo Da-young**
026 검은 방-**정지아** The Black Room-**Jeong Ji-a**
027 도쿄의 마야-**장류진** Maya in Tokyo-**Jang Ryu-jin**
028 홀리데이 홈-**편혜영** Holiday Home-**Pyun Hye-young**
029 해피 투게더-**서장원** Happy Together-**Seo Jang-won**
030 골드러시-**서수진** Gold Rush-**Seo Su-jin**
031 당신이 보고 싶어하는 세상-**장강명** The World You Want to See-**Chang Kang-myoung**
032 지난밤 내 꿈에-**정한아** Last Night, In My Dream-**Chung Han-ah**
Special 휴가중인 시체-**김중혁** Corpse on Vacation-**Kim Jung-hyuk**
Special 사파에서-**방현석** Love in Sa Pa-**Bang Hyeon-seok**

Through literature, you
bilingual Edition Modern

ASIA Publishers' carefully selected

Set 1

Division

Industrialization

Women

Set 2

Liberty

Love and Love

Affairs

South and North

Set 3

Seoul

Tradition

Avant-Garde

Set 4

Diaspora

Family

Humor

Search "bilingual edition

can meet the real Korea!
Korean Literature

22 keywords to understand Korean literature

Set 5
Relationships
Discovering
Everyday Life
Taboo and Desire

Set 6
Fate
Aesthetic Priests
The Naked in the
Colony

Set 7
Colonial Intellectuals Turned "Idiots"
Traditional Korea's Lost Faces
Before and After Liberation
Korea After the Korean War

korean literature"on Amazon!